Tom Turkey's Thanksgiving Trivia Challenge

More than 60 questions and answers about the Thanksgiving Holiday

Jonathan Ozanne

DEDICATION

For Sarah, Josiah and Gideon.

In memory of Micah.

CONTENTS

ACKNOWLEDGMENTS

The author is grateful for the encouragement he has received from his family and friends while writing this book.

INTRODUCTION

Thanksgiving is a fun, family-centered holiday. Since childhood it has been one of my favorite holidays. Thanksgiving is a common holiday around the world and different cultures have different ways of expressing thanks. This book is primarily about the American holiday known as Thanksgiving. The format of the book is fairly simple. First the questions, which have been arranged into different categories. After all of the questions have been asked, the next part of the book has the answers. A bibliography is at the back of the book. To keep score it is recommended that you write your answers (usually whether you chose answer A, B, or C for a particular question) on a piece of paper. Then when you get to the answer section, you can score your answers. The answers are given in some detail so you won't need to flip back to the questions to see what was being asked for a given question.

This book can be used to learn about Thanksgiving and it can also be used as a friendly or competitive group game to see who knows the most about Thanksgiving. I hope you have at least as much fun answering these questions as I had researching and writing them!

Jonathan Ozanne

QUESTIONS

MODERN THANKSGIVING

1. What is the main traditional dish at an American Thanksgiving Dinner?
   - A. Ham
   - B. Lamb
   - C. Turkey

2. Which of the following is not a traditional Thanksgiving food?
   - A. Cranberry sauce
   - B. Sweet potatoes
   - C. Mashed potatoes
   - D. Pumpkin pie
   - E. All of the above are traditional Thanksgiving foods

3. For many people part of the their Thanksgiving includes attending or watching the Macy's Thanksgiving Day Parade. When was the first Macy's Thanksgiving Day Parade?
   - A. 1904
   - B. 1924
   - C. 1944

4. What was the name of the character depicted on the first balloon float at the Macy's Parade?
   - A. Snoopy
   - B. Felix the Cat
   - C. Tintin

5. Watching a football game (or two) on television is a popular Thanksgiving Day activity. Playing on Thanksgiving has become a tradition for some teams. What year did the Detroit Lions first play a football game on Thanksgiving?
    A. 1914
    B. 1934
    C. 1954

6. When was the first college football game held on Thanksgiving?
    A. 1876
    B. 1926
    C. 1976

7. True or False? The Wednesday before Thanksgiving is a surprisingly light travel day?

8. When does the custom of visiting family on Thanksgiving date from?
    A. Early 1700s
    B. Early 1800s
    C. Early 1900s

9. What is one reason that people in some parts of the United States eat fried turkey rather than baked turkey on Thanksgiving?
    A. Thanksgiving Dinner does not have enough calories and so frying the turkey helps give the calorie count a little nudge
    B. Eating fried turkey is more common in warmer regions where baking a turkey for several hours can make a home unbearably warm
    C. Reliable oven repairmen are not found everywhere and so in these regions frying food is preferred.

10. Which of the following inventions had the most impact on the foods eaten at Thanksgiving Dinner?
    A. Refrigeration
    B. Canning
    C. Television

11. Since approximately when has Thanksgiving marked the "official" start of the Christmas shopping season?
    A. 1860s
    B. 1920s
    C. 1950s

12. The Pilgrims sailed across the Atlantic in 1620 on the now-famous ship the Mayflower. Originally the trip was to be made with another ship, but that ship sprang a leak off the coast of England and everyone crowded aboard the Mayflower. What was the name of the leaky boat that had to return to England?
    A. Fair Maiden
    B. Bon Homme Richard
    C. Speedwell

13. What famous legal document did the Pilgrims draft on the Mayflower before coming ashore in America?
    A. Articles of Confederation
    B. Magna Carta
    C. Mayflower Compact

14. What was the name of the place that the Pilgrims settled in 1620?
    A. Roanoke
    B. Jamestown
    C. Plymouth

15. True or False? The dark somber clothes with lots of buckles is an accurate representation of what the Pilgrims wore?

16. Which of the following locations does not have a competing claim for the site of the First Thanksgiving in the U.S.?
    A. El Paso, Texas
    B. Santa Fe, New Mexico
    C. Saint Augustine, Florida
    D. Jamestown, Virginia
    E. Augusta, Maine

17. What Native American tribe participated in the First Thanksgiving?
    A. Hassanamisco
    B. Naumkeag
    C. Wampanoag

18. What was the name of the leader or sachem who attended the first Thanksgiving?
    A. Massasoit
    B. Philippe
    C. Gray Fox

19. How did Squanto help the colonists?
    A. Hunting food for them
    B. Interpreter and technical advisor
    C. He warned of an attack by the Narragansett

20. True or False? Forks were among the eating utensils at the First Thanksgiving?

21. True or False? Deer were eaten at the First Thanksgiving?

22. True or False? Popcorn was eaten at the First Thanksgiving?

23. Which of the following was not eaten at the First Thanksgiving?
    A. Cranberry sauce
    B. Sweet potatoes
    C. Mashed potatoes
    D. Pumpkin pie
    E. All of the above were eaten at the First Thanksgiving
    F. None of the above were eaten at the First Thanksgiving

24. Which early colonist's writings provide one of the few written records of life at Plymouth Colony?
    A. Miles Standish
    B. William Bradford
    C. Zebulon Pike

25. What is the most likely month in which the First Thanksgiving was held?
    A. September
    B. October
    C. November

26. What is Plymouth Rock?
    A. A large obsidian outcropping that rises out of Cape Cod near Plymouth
    B. The name of the jail at Plymouth Colony. Miles Standish was briefly jailed there for dancing
    C. A large granite boulder of legendary status that achieved fame more than 100 years after the arrival at Plymouth

HISTORY OF THANKSGIVING

27. True or False? Giving thanks for a plentiful harvest is an ancient custom?

28. The ancient Greeks and Romans had Fall harvest festivals. When did the ancient Egyptians have their harvest festival?
    A. Spring
    B. Summer
    C. Fall
    D. Winter

29. How old is the custom of making a wish on the wishbone after the turkey has been eaten?
    A. It has been around since Ancient Rome
    B. It has been around since the Middle Ages
    C. It has been around since Victorian times

30. A horn of plenty or cornucopia (a large horn depicted overflowing with harvest bounty) has been around since the time of the Ancient Greeks. How long has it been a symbol of Thanksgiving?
    A. It has been a symbol of Thanksgiving since Ancient Rome
    B. It has been a symbol of Thanksgiving since the Middle Ages
    C. It has been a symbol of Thanksgiving since Victorian times

31. What is the source of the name turkey?
    A. The Middle Eastern nation with the same name
    B. Christopher Columbus
    C. A corruption of a native word

32. When Thanksgiving began to be observed on an annual basis in New England (generally the 1700s), how much church attendance was part of the observance?
    A. The day was dominated by two worship services with only a brief meal in-between
    B. One church service of a few hours length
    C. Generally people did not attend church on Thanksgiving

33. What author and ladies' journal editor campaigned for years (17 to 36 depending on sources) to establish Thanksgiving as a national holiday?
    A. Harriet Beecher Stowe
    B. Sarah Josepha Hale
    C. Louisa May Alcott

34. What 19th century president declared a National Day of Thanksgiving?
    A. James Monroe
    B. Abraham Lincoln
    C. Grover Cleveland

35. Which president attempted to move Thanksgiving to November 23rd in order to lengthen the Christmas shopping season?
    A. Franklin Roosevelt
    B. Richard Nixon
    C. Gerald Ford

36. True or False? During World War II, many soldiers ate better Thanksgiving Dinners than their families back home?

37. What year did the National Turkey Federation first give the president a turkey?
    A. 1937
    B. 1947
    C. 1957

38. Although many presidents are associated with the first presidential pardon of a turkey, who was the first president to issue an official pardon to a turkey?
    A. Abraham Lincoln
    B. John F. Kennedy
    C. George H.W. Bush

39. What state was the first to make Thanksgiving a holiday?
    A. New Hampshire
    B. New York
    C. Washington

40. When did Thanksgiving become an annual national holiday?
    A. 1677
    B. 1789
    C. 1863

THANKSGIVING FOODS

41. What breed of turkey is the one most commonly consumed on Thanksgiving?
    A. Large White
    B. Narragansett
    C. Bourbon Red
    D. American Bronze
    E. Jersey Buff

42. What dish is popular in Baltimore, Maryland as a regional Thanksgiving treat?
    A. Sauerkraut
    B. Pumpernickel
    C. Grits

43. What locally produced nut is often substituted for pecans or walnuts at Thanksgiving Dinner in Washington?
    A. Peanut
    B. Hazelnut
    C. Chestnut

44. Which of the following foods originally was associated with Christmas feasting but was added to Thanksgiving by Puritans who did not observe Christmas?
    A. Ham
    B. Mincemeat pie
    C. Candied yams

45. What state produces the most cranberries?
    A. Michigan
    B. Oregon
    C. Wisconsin

46. True or False? Ripe cranberries bounce when dropped on a hard surface?

47. What state produces the most pumpkins?
    A. California
    B. Illinois
    C. Pennsylvania

48. What state produces the most sweet potatoes?
    A. Louisiana
    B. Mississippi
    C. North Carolina

49. What state produces the most turkeys?
    A. Arkansas
    B. Minnesota
    C. North Carolina

50. On average, about how many turkeys are consumed at Thanksgiving?
    A. 30 million
    B. 45 million
    C. 60 million

51. True or False? Wild turkeys can fly?

52. True or False? Farm-raised turkeys can fly?

53. What year was the first commercial tofu turkey-substitute available?
    A. 1972
    B. 1982
    C. 1992

54. Which meat is not in Turducken?
    A. Ham
    B. Duck
    C. Chicken

55. When was Green Bean Casserole invented?
    A. Before 1850
    B. Between 1850 and 1950
    C. After 1950

56. Marshmallows were invented in the early 1800s. When were they first used in sweet potato casserole?
    A. 1820s
    B. 1880s
    C. 1920s

57. When did pies become part of the Thanksgiving Dinner?
    A. 1600s
    B. 1700s
    C. 1800s

58. When was the first can of Libby's pumpkin sold?
    A. 1909
    B. 1929
    C. 1949

59. What type of pie is common on Thanksgiving Dinner tables in Florida?
    A. Orange Crème
    B. Key Lime
    C. Grapefruit Express

THANKSGIVING AROUND THE WORLD

60. When is Thanksgiving in Canada?
    A. Second Monday in October
    B. Fourth Thursday in October
    C. Fourth Thursday in November

61. When is the Harvest Home held in Britain?
    A. September
    B. October
    C. Depends on the Harvest Moon

62. What is the name of the Jewish harvest festival?
    A. Sukkot
    B. Yom Kippur
    C. Hanukkah

63. When is the Hindu harvest festival of *Pongal*?
    A. January 14
    B. November 14
    C. December 14

64. What is the name of a special pastry served at a Chinese Thanksgiving?
    A. Sun cake
    B. Moon cake
    C. Jade cake

65. In Japan, a festival called *Niiname-Sai*, held November 23, was originally dedicated to _____ and the nature of the holiday has changed to become more like a day of Thanksgiving?
    A. Cranes
    B. The Emperor
    C. Buddha

66. Known as *Chusok*, what day is the Korean harvest festival?
    A. August 15
    B. October 15
    C. November 15

67. Literally going around (orbiting) the world, when was the first Thanksgiving in Outer Space?
    A. 1963
    B. 1973
    C. 1983

ANSWERS

MODERN THANKSGIVING

1. C. Turkey is the main traditional dish at an American Thanksgiving Dinner. Ham or lamb are more common at a Canadian Thanksgiving Dinner.

2. E. Cranberries, potatoes, sweet potatoes, and pie are all traditional Thanksgiving foods.

3. B. The first Macy's Thanksgiving Day Parade was held in 1924 in New York City.

4. B. Felix the Cat was the first character depicted on a balloon float in the Macy's Parade.

5. B. The Detroit Lions first played on Thanksgiving in 1934. Their opponent was the Chicago Bears. The Bears won 19-16. The Dallas Cowboys also traditionally play football on Thanksgiving.

6. A. The first college football game held on Thanksgiving was in 1876. It was the Intercollegiate Football Association championship. It was held at the Polo Grounds in New York City. Yale defeated Princeton.

7. False. The day before Thanksgiving is one of the busiest travel days of the year.

8. B. Since the early 1800s it has been traditional to visit extended family on Thanksgiving.

9. B. Fried turkey is more common in warmer regions of the United States. This is in part because baking a turkey for several hours can make a home unbearably warm.

10. A. Refrigeration has made it easier to eat a wider variety of food at cheaper prices on Thanksgiving. Refrigeration has had a greater impact on the foods eaten at Thanksgiving than canning or television. By analyzing cookbooks and cultural magazines, historians have shown that Thanksgiving Dinner menus became much more diversified starting in the 1950s. This diversity coincides with the availability of cheap, year-round refrigeration. Refrigeration also helps keep the leftovers from Thanksgiving Dinner fresh.

11. B. Christmas presents became common in the 1870s. By the 1920s there was a concerted effort by retailers to maximize the Christmas shopping season. The Macy's Thanksgiving Parade is an example of tying Thanksgiving to Christmas shopping. Recently many retailers are choosing to remain open on Thanksgiving Day. There has been a mixed reaction to this decision. Of course other retailers are closed on Thanksgiving but have had Christmas-themed items on their store shelves since September. Not everyone approves of the commercialization of Christmas or the lengthening of the shopping season. The commercialization of Christmas has been decried since at least the 1850s. A few years after the First Thanksgiving, in 1627, the Puritans in America and England began banning the celebration of Christmas. (For lots more trivia about Christmas, see my book *Santa Claus's Christmas Trivia Challenge*)

THANKSGIVING IN 1621

12. C. The Speedwell was the name of the ship that was going to accompany the Mayflower but had to transfer her passengers to the Mayflower and return to England because of a leak. Of the passengers on the Mayflower, about half were fleeing religious persecution and the other half were coming to the New World to seek their fortune. Most famous among the fortune-seekers was Captain Miles Standish, hired to lead a small group of soldiers to provide security for the Pilgrims. Most histories including this one tend to use the term Pilgrim to refer to the colonists on the Mayflower even if that term is not technically the most accurate.

13. C. The Mayflower went off course during the voyage. It was supposed to land at an existing colony near what is now New York City about two hundred miles away from where the Pilgrims actually landed. As noted in the answer to question 12, there was some diversity among the passengers in terms of their beliefs, goals, and motivations for coming to America. Given these factors, the passengers prudently drew up a plan of governance, known as the Mayflower Compact.

14. C. The famous Pilgrims, Puritans from England by way of the Netherlands, settled in Plymouth, Massachusetts in December, 1620. (Sometimes spelled Plimouth). Plymouth was founded on the ruins of a recently abandoned Indian village called Patuxet. Patuxet was abandoned when nearly the whole village was struck down by smallpox. Squanto was one of the few survivors. The survivors had moved to another village by the time the Pilgrims arrived.

15. False. Recent scholarship has shown that the Pilgrims wore colorful clothes. The myth that the Pilgrims wore somber clothes is a 19th century invention.

16. E. Augusta, Maine does not have a competing claim for the site of the First Thanksgiving. The other locations given (El Paso, Santa Fe, Saint Augustine, and Jamestown) do not even represent a complete list of known places that had some sort of ceremony "giving thanks" that could be called a "thanksgiving", that occurred prior to the Plymouth Thanksgiving of 1621. Since 1841, the Plymouth Thanksgiving has been known nationally as the site of the First Thanksgiving. It has also been since 1841 that Pilgrims and turkeys have been associated with Thanksgiving.

17. C. The Wampanoag tribe participated in the First Thanksgiving. Early accounts (and many school textbooks of yesteryear) fail to emphasize how crucial the assistance of the Wampanoag was to the survival of Plymouth. In particular, what the Wampanoag taught the colonists about local agriculture was vital for their survival. (European methods of agriculture that the colonists tried were unsuccessful). More recent histories tend to fail to emphasize that the colonists were not without power. In 1621 the Wampanoag needed the colonists and the colonists needed the Wampanoag. The First Thanksgiving can be viewed as a celebration but also as an attempt by two different groups of people to forge a more friendly and cooperative relationship. (Unfortunately the cooperation did not last and about 50 years after the First Thanksgiving, the descendants fought a violent war that ended very badly for the Wampanoag, who lost a great deal of territory and power).

18. A. Massasoit was the leader or sachem of the Wampanoag. Although he did not entirely trust the Pilgrims, he sought an alliance with them in part because the Wampanoag had been weakened by the smallpox plague of a few years earlier. Some estimates are that more than 75% of the Wampanoag were killed by smallpox a few years before the Pilgrims arrived.

19. B. Squanto helped the colonists as an interpreter and technical advisor. He taught them how to plant corn and about the local flora and fauna. Squanto, also known as Tisquantum, played a crucial role in attempting to foster peaceful cooperation because he spoke English and had previously been to England. A few years earlier, against his will, he was captured by a slave trader and taken to England but he escaped and returned to America, where he discovered that his village had been decimated by smallpox.

20. False. Forks did not become eating utensils until the 1700s, about a hundred years after the First Thanksgiving.

21. True. Deer were eaten at the First Thanksgiving. The deer would have been considered a delicacy by both the Native Americans and the colonists. The Wampanoag brought five deer to the First Thanksgiving to the delight of the Pilgrims.

22. True. Popcorn was eaten at the First Thanksgiving.

23. F. None of the above. Cranberry sauce, sweet potatoes, mashed potatoes, and pumpkin pie were all later additions to the Thanksgiving menu.

24. B. William Bradford, the second governor of Plymouth, wrote about his experiences and his writings provide an important record of life at Plymouth Colony.

25. B. The first Thanksgiving was most likely held in October of 1621. The precise date is unknown.

26. C. Plymouth Rock is reported to be the place where the Pilgrims arrived at Plymouth. This arrival is based on second-hand accounts in 1741 from a descendant of an original colonist.

HISTORY OF THANKSGIVING

27. True. Celebrating a successful crop or a successful harvest or deliverance from some calamity is an ancient custom, observed in many different cultures. In England, the Harvest Home festival in celebration of the harvest was observed in England in the 1600s. It is still celebrated today.

28. A. The Egyptians celebrated the harvest in the Spring.

29. A. The custom of breaking the wishbone of a turkey by having two people break it, with the person who has a larger piece being granted one wish (similar to wishing on a star) is at least as old as the Ancient Romans. (At least a couple hundred years B.C.)

30. C. Cornucopias have been symbols of Thanksgiving since Victorian times. In Greek mythology, the cornucopia magically produced ambrosia and nectar.

31. A. Turkeys are native to the southern United States and Mexico. They had been discovered by the early Spanish

explorers and brought back to Europe in the 1500s. Merchants from Turkey were early dealers in these birds, and the source of the name according to the Oxford English Dictionary. B and C are plausible answers. Columbus was notorious for seeing everything through the lens of having made it to the East Indies. He is alleged to have named turkeys after the East Indian word for peacock (*tuka*). A Native American word for turkey is close to turkey (*firkee*).

32. A. Originally Thanksgiving was dominated by all-day services with only a brief meal. The First Thanksgiving lasted three days and was a secular event. The Second Thanksgiving, held in 1623 to give thanks for the end of a drought, was mostly a religious event.

33. B. Sarah Josepha Hale campaigned tirelessly for decades and was ultimately successful in getting Thanksgiving turned into a national holiday.

34. B. In 1863, Abraham Lincoln declared a National Day of Thanksgiving on the last Thursday of November. He did this Thanksgiving declaration in response to the efforts of Sarah Josepha Hale. Thanksgiving was also observed in the South prior to the Civil War, so the divisive Civil War was not an obstacle to Thanksgiving becoming a national holiday.

35. A. In 1939 Franklin Roosevelt attempted to move Thanksgiving to a fixed date of November 23. The theory was that this would boost retail sales by generally lengthening the Christmas shopping season. This date change was derisively named "Franksgiving". Many states observed Thanksgiving on the customary date of the last Thursday of the month rather than on Franksgiving. Two years later Roosevelt admitted his mistake and signed

legislation that set Thanksgiving as the fourth Thursday in November.

36. True. In an effort to boost morale, or at least preventing it from sagging, the U.S. armed forces went to great effort to get Thanksgiving Dinners to troops. Ironically, family back home may have eaten a lesser dinner owing to shortages and rationing.

37. B. In 1947 the National Turkey Federation gave a few turkeys to President Truman. Every year since then, it has given the current president a similar gift.

38. C. The first president to issue a formal pardon to a turkey was George H.W. Bush in 1989. Pardoning a turkey at Thanksgiving has been an annual tradition since then. Presidents most often incorrectly credited with issuing the first turkey pardon include: Lincoln, Truman, Kennedy, and Reagan.

39. B. New York was the first state to make Thanksgiving an annual state holiday, doing so in 1817. Prior to Thanksgiving becoming a state holiday, in many states, many people still celebrated it even though it was not legally recognized as an official holiday. The celebrations varied from state to state whether they were annual or on an irregular basis. The celebrations also varied whether they were mostly secular or mostly religious in nature.

40. C. Thanksgiving has been an annual national holiday since 1863. Prior to 1863 occasionally national days of Thanksgiving would be declared, such as in 1777 during the American War of Independence after the victory at Saratoga. George Washington issued two National Day of Thanksgiving proclamations during his presidency. Some people argued against Thanksgiving as an annual holiday,

arguing that it should only be held when people were truly thankful. Between 1621 and 1863 Thanksgiving went from being an infrequent regional holiday to an annual national holiday.

THANKSGIVING FOODS

41. A. Large White is the breed of turkey most commonly consumed on Thanksgiving. The other breeds mentioned more closely resemble the turkeys found in North America in the 1600s. Large Whites are raised particularly to be eaten.

42. A. Sauerkraut is a traditional Thanksgiving side dish in Baltimore, Maryland.

43. B. Hazelnuts are often part of Thanksgiving Dinner in Washington. They are often substituted for pecans or walnuts.

44. B. Mincemeat pie was (and is) associated with Christmas. When the Puritans banned Christmas celebrations, mincemeat pie became part of the Thanksgiving Dinner menu for many.

45. C. Wisconsin produces the most cranberries. Massachusetts is second.

46. True. Ripe cranberries bounce when dropped on a hard surface.

47. B. Illinois produces most of the pumpkins grown in the United States. Most production takes place within a 90 mile radius of Peoria, Illinois. California is a distant second in pumpkin production.

48. C. North Carolina produces the most sweet potatoes. However, China is the leading producer of sweet potatoes accounting for more than 80% of sweet potato production. The United States only produces about 1% of global sweet potato production.

49. B. Minnesota produces the most turkeys. North Carolina comes in a close second.

50. B. Around 45 million turkeys on average are consumed at Thanksgiving.

51. True. Wild turkeys can fly, although they generally do not fly far on any given flight.

52. False. Farm-raised turkeys are unable to fly.

53. C. The first commercial turkey-substitute made from tofu became available in 1992. Tofu turkey was invented by Gary Abramowitz and sold by Fresh Tofu, Inc.

54. A. Of the choices given, ham is not usually found in turducken. Turducken is made of turkey, duck, and chicken. It is a Cajun dish and is popular in Louisiana. Retired football announcer and former coach John Madden was noted for being a turducken aficionado.

55. C. Green Bean Casserole was invented in 1955. The casserole is very popular around Thanksgiving, Christmas and Easter. The popularity of Green Bean Casserole noticeably drives up sales of other ingredients in the casserole at those times (for example, French's Fried Onions).

56. C. Marshmallows were first used in sweet potato casserole in the 1920s. Marshmallow candy has been around since the early 1800s. Originally marshmallows included the marshmallow plant hence the name. Marshmallows are still called marshmallows even though they are no longer made from marshmallows.

57. C. Pies became a staple of Thanksgiving Dinner in the 1800s when more homes had easy access to the ovens necessary to bake them.

58. B. The first can of Libby's pumpkin was sold in 1929. For many people, Thanksgiving is not complete without a slice or two of pumpkin pie.

59. B. Key Lime pie is a popular Thanksgiving treat in Florida.

THANKSGIVING AROUND THE WORLD

60. A. The second Monday in October is celebrated as Thanksgiving in Canada. Thanksgiving was established as an official holiday in Canada in 1957.

61. C. The Harvest Home is held on the Sunday closest to the Harvest Moon. This is usually in September but can be in early October.

62. A. Sukkot (soo-KOTE), also known as the Feast of the Tabernacles, is the name of the Jewish harvest festival. It is held in September or October each year.

63. A. The Hindu harvest festival of *Pongal* is on January 14.

64. B. Moon cakes are served at a Chinese Thanksgiving.

65. B. The *Niiname-Sai* festival, once dedicated to the Emperor, has since 1948 been turned into a day like Thanksgiving.

66. A. *Chusok*, the Korean Harvest Festival which is also honors ancestors, is on August 15.

67. B. The first Thanksgiving in space was at the Skylab space station in 1973 with astronauts Gerald Carr, Edward Gibson, and William Pogue. It has been celebrated in space several times since then.

SCORING

Generally more than 50% correct is a good score. Feel free to raise or lower your standards.

Regardless of how many you got correct, I hope these questions were fun and prompt you to learn more about Thanksgiving!

BIBLIOGRAPHY AND SUGGESTED RESOURCES

Anderson, Laurie Halse. *Thank You, Sarah : the woman who saved Thanksgiving.* New York : Simon and Schuster, 2002.

Baker, James W. *Thanksgiving : The biography of an American holiday.* Lebanon, NH : University Press of New England, 2009.

Bleier, Edward. *The Thanksgiving Ceremony : New Traditions for America's family feast.* New York : Crown Publishers, 2003.

Brown, Leslie. *The new shorter Oxford English dictionary on historical principles.* Oxford : Clarendon Press, 1993.

Colman, Penny. *Thanksgiving : The true story.* New York : Henry Holt and Company, 2008.

Gibbons, Gail. *Thanksgiving is....* New York : Holiday House, 2004.

Grace, Catherine O'Neill. *1621 : a new look at Thanksgiving.* Washington D.C. : National Geographic Society, 2001.

Greenwood, Barbara. *A pioneer Thanksgiving : a story of harvest celebrations in 1841.* Tonawanda, NY : Kids Can Press Ltd., 1999.

Heinrichs, Ann. *Thanksgiving.* Mankato, MN : The Child's World, 2014.

Hillstrom, Laurie Collier. *Thanksgiving : The American Holiday.* Detroit, MI : Omnigraphics, 2011.

Kule, Elaine A. *Celebrate Thanksgiving Day.* Berkeley Heights, NJ : Enslow Publishers, Inc., 2006.

Merrick, Patrick. *Thanksgiving Turkeys.* Mankato, MN : The Child's World, 2000.

Nelson, Robin. *Thanksgiving.* Minneapolis, MN : Lerner Publications Company, 2010.

Sloate, Susan. *Pardon that Turkey : How Thanksgiving became a holiday*. New York : Grosset & Dunlap, 2010.

Trueit, Trudi Strain. *Thanksgiving*. New York : Children's Press, 2007.

WEBSITES

http://www.agmrc.org/commodities__products/livestock/poultry/turkey-profile/

http://www.agmrc.org/commodities__products/fruits/cranberries/

http://www.agmrc.org/commodities__products/vegetables/pumpkins/

http://www.agmrc.org/commodities__products/vegetables/sweet-potato-profile/

ABOUT THE AUTHOR

The author is a lawyer who lives with his family near St. Paul, Minnesota. Some of the other quiz books he has written are: *Santa Claus's Christmas Trivia Challenge: 100 questions about the secular and sacred customs of Christmas, Easter Trivia Challenge* and *George Washington's Monumental Presidential Trivia Challenge : More 500 questions about the 44 U.S. Presidents from Washington to Obama.*

70761556R00024

Made in the USA
Lexington, KY
15 November 2017